POGO'S DOUBLE SUNDAE

Two unabridged helpings of past Pogo classics

BY WALT KELLY

The Pogo Sunday Parade

The Pogo Sunday Brunch

A Fireside Book Published by Simon and Schuster

Published by Simon and Schuster
A Division of Gulf & Western Corporation
Simon & Schuster Building, Rockefeller Center
1230 Avenue of the Americas, New York, New York 10020
FIRESIDE and colophon are registered trademarks of Simon & Schuster

Designed by Helen Barrow
Manufactured in the United States of America

6 7 8 9 10 11 12

Library of Congress Catalog Card No. 77-16729
ISBN 0-671-24139-7

CONTENTS

THE POGO SUNDAY PARADE

THE POGO SUNDAY BRUNCH

THE POGO
SUNDAY PARADE

The POGO
SUNDAY
PARADE

Dedication

For Ruth, David, Kenny
And Ann and the many
Others plus Peter
And Tony (who's sweeter
than tooth paste) and Steven
And Andrew and even
The Oho, the Kit Kat
And that's about that....
Except, of course, Paul.....
Is that really all?

Back to Earth

Our story opens on the dark side of the moon where a small group of scientists plan to return to Earth bringing with them the secrets of the Universe, the chart of the stars, the keys to the Heavens.

16

18

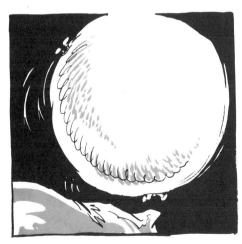

23

High G Over Whiz

Where the River wetful winds
The Spring doth spring
and Fall
Becomes the Sum or total
All
Of Winter's mournful minds.
Mind the children soon
or late
And whistle in the dog;
There is no thaw, thin ice
or fog
Nor thrift in fifty-eight.

A Roaming Candle

Rabbits are rounder
Than Bandicoots, Sam.
A Bunny's a Bounder
In old Alabam.

Thus is the Thistle
The thrush of the Thick,
And wet is the whistle
That winnows the wick.

ONE SUNDAY MORN
AT BREAK OF BORN

Bacon and eggs
And pieces of pie,
Blue is my love
And red is her eye,
Purple her hair
As deep as the sky,
Hello there, Myrtle,
Hello and Goodbye.

WOWF

34

LOOKY THERE! YO' MANAGER GOT INTO MY SECRET CACHE OF SAM'ITCHES--AN' IS ET ALL OF 'EM.

OOG.

YOU SHOUNTNA KEP' 'EM IN THE WETWASH.

HOWDJA LIKE THE LIVERWURST AN' HONEY KIND?

WHEN I SAYS "OOG!" DOES THAT SUGGEST ANYTHIN'?

YOU DON'T GOTTA BE SO SMART--YOU ET PART OF THE WASH TOO--MR.GRIZZLE BEAR GOT TWO UNDERWEARS AND A SOCK MISSIN'!

YOU BETTER GIT MOVIN' BEFORE OL' BEAR MOVES YOU.

OOG I CAN'T MOVE.

POOR THING--- HE'S SICK! WE'LL TOTE HIM IN THE BASKET.

HOT DOG! I LOVES BASKET RIDES.

HE AIN'T HALF AS SICK AS ME-- JES' LOOKIN' AT HIM RIDIN' MAKES ME SICK.

JES' LOOKIN' AT YOU DOIN' ANYTHIN' AIN'T EXACTLY A CURE-ALL.

36

37

DOWN TO BEAR AND BRASSY FACTS

WAIT A JES' A **DOGBONE** MINUTE --- DOES YOU MEAN **ME** WHOM OR **HIM** WHOM---? **WHO** WHOM?

YEAH!

OWL WHOM! **THAT'S** THE WHO WHOM WHOM IS WHO---!

ON ACCOUNT OF **HOWLAND *WHO* OWL** IS THE CRITTUR WHAT ET THE HOLE IN YO' CAMISOLE AN' *DEE-*VOURED YO' PANTY-WAIST! *J'ACCUSE!*

DON'T YOU CALL **ME** NO **J'ACCUSE!**

NOW TAKE IT EASY, FRIEND--- HE IS **FEARLESS CON-FESSIN'** YO' **GUILT**---GIVE HIM CREDICK!

J'ACCUSE! J'ACCUSE! J'ACCUSE!

I IS JES' HAD A QUIETLY BEAUTIFUL THOUGHT---'LONG AS THEM CLOES IS *YOURN,* MR. GRIZZLE BEAR, WHY NOT MAKE A AUTOPSY ON *YOU?*

IT'S ONLY FAIR--- THE AMERICAN WAY IS BEST.

THE LITTLE **WHIPPERSNACKER** THERE GOT A VERY SOUND **LEGAL** POINT.

WHIPPER-WHAT?

HAW!

IS YOU DISPUTIN' MY FRIEND'S **LEGAL POINT**? WHAT'S YOU SAYIN' "**HAW**" AT?

AT **YOU** IS WHAT I'M SAYIN' IT AT----

PHOO!

STEP OUT HERE AN' SAY THAT, FRIEND.

FRIEND BEAR, TURTLE IS RIGHT--- IF YOU WAS THE OWNER OF THE **CONSUMED SMALL CLO'ES**--THEN--

DON'T BOTHER ME, I IS WAITIN' FOR TURTLE TO STEP OUT LIKE A MAN.

BUT I **INSIST**-- IF THAT'S THE CASE, OUR TROUBLES ARE OVER!

HIS TROUBLES AIN'T OVER --- HE INSULTED ME AN' I GONE HANG 'ROUND OUTSIDE FER HIM.

YESSIR--- OUR TROUBLES ARE OVER -- **WE'LL MAKE MILLIONS** AN' LIVE LIKE **KINGS**.

HUH?

LIKE **QUEENS**, EVEN.

51

54

FOR A **MINUTE** I THUNK HE WAS GONE **COTCH** US AN' **EAT** US AN' **ME** *WITH NO CEMETERY PLOT.*

UNCLE SASSAFRASH **ALLUS** SAID A BOY OUGHT TO BUY HISSELF A **BURYIN' PLOT** WITH HIS **FIRST DOLLAR.**

BUT, IF THAT **MONSTER** ET YOU AN' ME, WE WOULDN'T OF **NEEDED** NO **CEMETERY PLOT** --- WE'D OF BEEN **OUT** A DOLLAR **EACH.**

HOWEVER, IF THE **MONSTER** HAD A **BURYIN' PLOT,** US WOULD OF ALL BEEN **INTERRED TOGETHER** SOONER OR LATER --- MORE OR LESS --AN' US WOULD OF **SAVED TWO BUCKS.**

AW-- THERE'S NO **FUTURE** IN SUCH INVESTMINTS.

I GUESS YOU'RE RIGHT-- ---IT'S A INVESTMINT FROM WHAT YOU WOULDN'T WANT **NO RETURNS** -- --THERE IS **NO** FUTURE IN BEIN' DEAD.

Y'KNOW IF UNCLE SASSAFRASH KNEW THAT HE'D **TURN IN** HIS **GRAVE.**

THE QUESTION IS --- *WHAT WOULD HE TURN IT IN FOR?*

58

60

66

MY SAKES! WHEN YOU PULLED OUT OL' BEAR, YOU PULLED OFF HIS PANTS!

HE LOOK A LI'L' *REE*-DICKLEMUST.

OUT OF DECENCY US OUGHT TO DREDGE OUT HIS PANTS.

LET'S NOT BE HASTY.... WE IS ALREADY PUT IN A HARD MORNING WORK.

LET US *SAUNTER* ON HOME FOR *LUNCH* AFTER WHICH US WILL RETURN WITH *PITCHFORKS, CROWBARS* AN' MEBBE A LI'L' *GUNPOWDER* AN' US WILL *PRY* THE BOY OUTEN THERE!

LIKE THE *GOOD NEIGHBORS* US IS.

LOOKY THERE, POGO, SOMEBODY WAS FIXIN' TO *COOK* A *GRIZZLE BEAR.*

?

WHOEVER PICKED THIS BEAR OUT‥PICKED A GOOD ONE‥ NICE AN' PLUMP———*HOWEVER,* YOU NOTICE IT AIN'T BEEN *SKUN*‥‥THAT AIN'T HARDLY THE WAY TO COOK A *GRIZZLE BEAR.*

JES' GIMME A LI'L' *BOOSK* UP AN' MEBBE I KIN HELP THOSE PEOPLE OUT A LI'L' BIT.

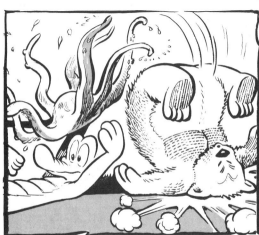

I SEES SOMETHIN'!

WOOP! THAT WASN'T MY PANTS--!

AN' IT SEES ME.

YOU GOT IT ON ME, YOU GIT IT OFF!

HALP! A RHINOCERWURST IS GOT ALBERT! HALP!

OCTOPOSSIBLE

78

FIGMENTALITY

CERT'LY -- YOU WOONENT WANT IT TO GIT THERE AFORE YOU, WOULD YOU?

YOU'RE SUCH A GOOD ADVISOR WHAT'D YOU TELL OL' ALBERT THERE TO DO?

MY LAND! I DON'T SEE ALBERT---BUT I'D ADVISE THAT YOUNG WOMAN OUT THERE TO GIVE UP SEE-GARS -- IT'S UNCOUTH!

THAT AIN'T UNCOUTH! THAT'S ALBERT!

BY JING! HE LOOK LIKE A SIGH-REEN!

YOU MEAN ONE OF THEM THINGS WHAT SIT ON THE FRONT OF A FIRE ENGINE?

NOPE---ONE OF THEM CRITTURS WHAT USED TO LURK IN THE LEGENDARY ISLANDS AN' LURED SAILORS TO THEY DEATHS.

I COMES FROM A SEA-FARIN' FAMBLY-- HE GOT SOME NERVE - HE'S A BEAST!

THAT'S WHAT HE LOOKS LIKE.

Really Round the Ragboys

Hobble the goblins
And rabble the rouse
Weary the Willie
And homily house
All of the Pollys
The Annas demand;
Deliver the liverty,
Bellow the Bland.

A Tuppenny Thrupence

Please plorridge hlot!
Please plorridge clold!
Please plorridge in the plot,
Nline dlays lold.

Our Colander is Full of Holes

The Firth of Forth
Lithe in the north,
The first of course
Comes 'fore the fourth
And after fourth is fifth,
Befourth, of course,
Forsooth the sixth;
With tooth and thirth
Somewheres betwixth
July the Forth and Firth.

A DILLER
A DULLARD
A TEN O'CLOCK
SKULLER

100

102

A DEEP IN THE SLEEP

105

SEE! GEORGIA IS PART OF THE U.S.S.R.

WHOOIE! DO YO' S'POSE SANDY CLAWS IS ON *THEIR* SIDE?

YOU FIGGER THEM **BOLSHEVINKS** CREPT UP AN' STOLT THE STATE?

THEY **MUST OF IS DO.**

MAPS PUZZLES AND OTHER MAGIC TRICKS

BY NAB! *THEY GOT A NERVE!*

YOU GOT A **SOAPBOX** ON YOU? I WANTS TO MAKE A SPEECH!

WE GOT NO TIME TO LOSE -- *US IS GOTTA STEAL BACK THE STATE!*

RIGHT! YOU JES' KEEP YO' ARMS OUT AN' I'LL FILL YOU UP--- THEN US WILL CRAWL *BACK* THRU THE HOLE!

BEARIN' OUR **BELOVED SWAMP** IN OUR ARMS!

US BETTER HURRY UP--- TAKE 'S MUCH 'S WE CAN.

I'LL BE DOGBONED IF *THEM* LI'L' *TOVAROOCHES* ISN'T STOLT OWL, TOO!

?

I DIN'T SEE THE EARLY PART OF THE SHOW; JES CAME IN---WHAT'S GOIN' ON, FRIEND?

WHERE IS *YOU* FROM, MR. HORNER?

I IS FROM OVER AT FARGO.

IT'S GOOD TO SEE A BOY FROM OVER AT HOME------WE GONE HAVE TROUBLE GITTIN' THE STATE BACK INTO THE U.S. AND A.

HUH?

ME AN'OWL DUG A HOLE THRU THE EARTH, COME OUT IN ROOSIA AN', *BEHOLD*, THEM BOLSHEVIKS HAD STOLED OUR SOVEREIGN STATE OF *GEORGIA*----THERE IT WAS **PLAIN** AS **MUD** ----

NEXT THING I KNEWED *OWL* HAD VANISHED AN'-

LISTEN! YOU AIN'T IN RUSSIA--- THIS IS ALL A **BAD** DREAM---YOU'RE HOME IN THE SWAMP---

TWO THREE MINUTE HEADS

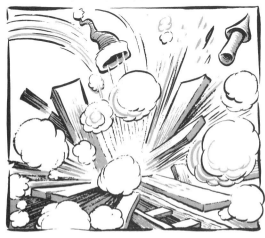

118

THOOD FOR FOUGHT!

121

124

125

126

SOB SOB!

HUSH YOUR LOUD SOBBIN'--YOU IS ONLY *ASSUMIN'* THERE *ISN'T NO VIRGINIA*, YO' NATIVE STATE AN' HOME TOWN.

I *BETS* YOU THERE ISN'T *NO VIRGINIA*-- THEM *BOLSHEVINKS* MUST IS STOLT *THAT'N* TOO.

PRIDE! PRIDE!

AS A OL' AN' *HONORABOBBLE SANDY CLAWS* I *BETS* YOU THAT BOLOGNA TO A MILLION DOLLARS I IS *RIGHT!*

SANDY, THAT'S A GOOD EVEN BET-- WAIT THERE.

BEHIND OF THIS *SCREEN* HE'LL NEVER SEE ME WRITIN' OUT THIS LETTER WHAT IS *SHEER PROOF!*

HERE'S DOCUMENT'RY EVIDENCE-- JES' IN FROM OL' JOHN COLBURN, IN RICHMOND. IT SAY: "*DEAR SANTA CLAUS: YES, THERE IS A VIRGINIA.*" REPEAT: "*DEAR SANTA CLAUS: YES, THERE IS A VIRGINIA!*"

I GUESS *THAT* REDUCES THE WHOLE ARGUMENT TO A MIZERBLE ABSURDIDITTY.

THAT'S THE WAY *I* FELT FINALLY--- SO WHILE YOU WAS *FORGIN'* THAT--- *I* ATE THE BOLOGNA.

SUIT'S A LI'L' SNUG BUT A GOOD LOOKIN' MAN MAKE A GOOD APPEARANCE IN **ANYTHING** HE THROW ON.

MAN! DIN'T THINK I'D GIT HERE IN TIME.

OL' BEAR

ONLY THOUGHTFUL FOLKS LIKE ME IS THOUGHTFUL -- THIS IS A GREAT IDEA TO PLAY SANDY CLAWS TO THE BEAR TADS. I DESERVE CREDIT, GREAT CREDIT.

THIS IS **MY** TERRITORY, FRIEND! **BACK OFF!**

WHEN **I** DISPENSES **BROTHERLY LOVE,** FRIEND --

NO DOGGONE BEAR IS GONE **STOP** ME!

WELCOME TO OUR **EASTER PARTY,** YOU **TWO OL' SANTY CLAUSES.**

EASTER PARTY?!

US LAID A EGG, B'RER RABBIT.

A Few Backwords

IT IS NOT so easy these days to sound a simple, clearheaded note of hysteria, but my friend Bill Vaughan, crafty columnist of the Kansas City *Star* and the NANA Service, working hand in glove with a certain cartoonist, is positive that the bugle with which to blow such a blast has been found.

Drift-finders, an organization devoted to the wetting of the wind with a forefinger, has discovered that the ordinary man in the street only appears to be smarter than his leaders both at home and abroad. In the January 1958 report, *Just Plumb Bob,* Mr. Vaughan indicates that there is every reason to believe that heads of government, statesmen, and other people with yellow briefcases and blue suits, are just playing at being stupid.

"If we are in a race with Russia," says Vaughan, "we cannot merely pretend to be stupid; we will have to be genuine idiots. WE MUST OUTSTUPEFY THE RUSSIANS."

That seems to be the key phrase: OUTSTUPEFY THE RUSSIANS. There is not much time left. But we have the material, the men, the know-how and somewhat of a tradition in the field.

In a letter to Mr. Vaughan outlining his thoughts on the subject, a dirt farmer in Dirt, New Braska, said: "My dirt crop isn't what it used to be, but, then, it never was. Trouble is with these government people. Most of them are half-bred idiots. What we have got to get is pure-bred idiots. I don't go for these new crops of idiots that got nothing like the stupidity of like when we were younger. I have found that

I get smarter as I get older, a condition that has done me no good in the party of my heart.

"You'll hear a lot of people tell you, 'The older I get the more stupid I get' or 'Shucks, the older I get the more stupid I get.' Some do it with a 'Shucks' and some do it raw, but it amounts to the same thing—pigwash. It's my belief and the belief of my sister's husband, Perle (he's the one with the mole), that this assumption of expanding ignorance is a pose and not a very graceful one at that.

"It's all right to strike an attitude of genius; that is every man's prerogative, like being born in a log cabin or burying your kin if they are dead. Anybody can pretend to be smart and get away with it, because, who is to say? But it takes the McCoy to pass yourself off as an ass or an idiot.

"Right there is where true blue blood counts. The blue corpuscles of the average idiot run very deep, in my opinion, and, I might add, Perle agrees. Right now we have got red corpuscles in the government and white corpuscles too, but the blue corpuscle is not represented there in the quantity that we think."

So ends the dirt farmer's letter. Most of us will probably agree that it is a brave and clarion call to increased brainlessness. There is some doubt that we will be able to reach our peak or even a reasonable stride in 1958. But there is no reason to think that we cannot all be numbskulls by 1959.

It is probably not too soon to warn again that our leaders in business, education and government are merely pretending to be stupid. As Mr. Vaughan suggests, we might give everyone a close check from now on. Genuine idiocy should be our goal. Remember, we must outstupefy the Russians in '59. There may be no '60. Rise, Dolts, you have nothing to lose but your brains.

THE POGO
SUNDAY BRUNCH

ᴛʜᴇ POGO
SUNDAY
BRUNCH

QUO VADIS?

This is a great era for those who are light of heart and hand. It is a period when the working funnyman can find material for the laugh (that revered ingredient of our communications systems, advertising media, Congressional bodies and the all but vanished smoking room) almost always at hand. If the boff does not spring out of the welter of haphazards that lay around in the mishmash of our daily lives, it can be stolen from friend or stranger because, no matter where we look, someone is trying to be funny.

There was a time when the funnyman was a rarity, a pride-giving product of the community. He was always named "Old Mert" or "Old Mort" or something like that, and if a Sunday afternoon proved dull beyond endurance, you could drive out to "Old Something's" place and watch him think up the funny ones. Those who assayed a sporadic raid (by use of a labored pun) upon this man's province were glared down by relatives on both sides. The funnyman was special. He was not the ordinary jay who walked with men.

Today those of us who cannot be funny singlehandedly repeat mirth-making anecdotes usually fitted with the best four-letter words that brains can buy. We also relate, with gestures, detailed descriptions of the last TV attack we had. We are a race in search of the joke. It occurs to a few that the greatest joke in the world is life itself, which, aside from being pleasant, full of hope, fears, sustained interest and laughs, finally winds up with a thing called death. Death is an essential part of life, like the laugh is part of the joke. It is a sort of recognizable ending.

It is really one more ridiculous facet of the joke, then, that we are so intent upon reaching the last laugh that a good many of us are fooling around with all sorts of means to the end. Perhaps we should enjoy more the telling of this tale, the living of this life and not hasten the arrival of the punch line. After our learning has set fire to the fuse of ignorance and we have finally blown the world into a billion funny pieces, what are we going to do for an encore?

But, enough of chuckles. Let us move into the serious part of the book.

A Rune Upon A Lunar Tune Aroon
(for Ellen)

The Moon is a Madness,
A Madness of mine.
I made her of mustard
And mulberry wine.

I garbed her in silver
And strawberry cheese
And halved her in quarters.
(Her quarters do please.)

I crowned her and gowned her
In Love all ashine,
So boot her and shoot her,
This Madness of mine.

A Sorry Soirée

I BEEN *STUDYIN'* AN' *A-STUDYIN'* THIS HERE *CHRISTMAS CAROL* WHAT GO ON ABOUT THEM *TWELVE DAYS OF CHRISTMAS*, AN' I DECLARE, FOR THE *SECOND* STRAIGHT YEAR, I IS STUMPED.

A *NEW RECORD.*

LOOKY HOW THIS FELLA *UPROOTS* A *PEAR TREE* AN' SENDS IT OFF TO HIS *TRUE LOVE* ··· ···THAT'S ON THE *FIRST* DAY.

NEXT DAY HE STUFFS TWO *TURTLE-DOVES* AND ANOTHER *PARTRIDGE* INTO ANOTHER PEAR TREE AN' HAULS *THAT* OVER TO HIS GAL'S HOUSE ··· LOOKS TO ME LIKE SHE STARTIN' EITHER A *FRUIT STAND* OR A *SCHOOL FOR BIRDS.*

NOT ONLY THAT, BUT THERE'S A INNOCENT *PARTRIDGE* LIVIN' IN THAT PEAR TREE ··· AN' YET THIS *LOVE-SICK LOLLYGAG* RIPS IT UP··· BIRD AN' ALL ··· MAKIN' *HIM* HOMELESS, AN' *SINGS* ABOUT IT ··· *GAY* AS CAN BE.

HOW WOULD *YOU* LIKE TO GET PEAR TREES, PARTRIDGES, AN' *TURTLE-DOVES* FOR *TWO DAYS'* HAND RUNNIN'?

IT AIN'T NOTHIN' I IS SET MY HEART ON.

THERE IT IS IN BLACK AN' WHITE. AN' ON THE *THIRD* DAY THIS *BIRD PLUCKER* SENDS OVER *THREE FRENCH HENS!*

FOREIGN CHICKENS!

THIS BOY DIN'T *LOVE* THIS GIRL -- HE *HATED* HER ... YOU EVER HEAR CHICKENS TALK? IT'S GABBLE GABBLE CLUCK CLUCK CLUCK ALL THE LIVIN' LONG DAY ... *IMAGINE HEARIN' THAT KINDA TALK IN FRENCH.*

IF *I* WAS THIS GIRL I'D SELL THIS GUY TO THE *TRAVELIN' GYPSIES* ... ...IF ANYBODY GIVES ME ANY POULTRY WHAT PUTS OUT A LOT OF *HINKY DINKY POLLY VOO*, MORNIN', NOON AN' NIGHT. THEY *DON'T GIT MY HAND IN MARRIAGE.* AN' YOU CAN PUT *THAT* IN YOUR PIPE AN' SMOKE IT.

I'LL MAKE A NOTE.

FAR'S *I* KIN FIGGER OUT, THIS BOY IN "TWELVE DAYS OF CHRISTMAS" WAS A *BURGLAR* AN' HIS GIRL FRIEND WAS A *FENCE* ... NOT ONLY DID HE SEND OVER ALL THEM FOWL, BUT HE SENT *RINGS, MUSICIANS* AND ...

MY SAKES, POGO, IT'S GETTIN' *LATE* -- ...YOU BETTER GIT ON HOME ...AN' *STOP USIN' MY TOOTH-BRUSH LEFT-HANDED!*

141

142

The Girl with the Churl

144

146

147

148

I DON'T KNOW WHAT TO THINK...

Still Secrets Run Deep

IS POGO MARRIED TO *ALBERT*?... HIM, AS WAS IN THE PEEK-A-BUNNY GOWN, OR IS THE ALBERT I KNOWS BEEN REPLACED BY A FEMALE TYPE?

AND WHAT WAS *CHURCHY* HIDIN' UNDER THE BED FOR? *IS IT POSSIBLE A ETERNAL TRIANGLE IS REARED ITS UGLY HEAD?* OH, I AM A CAD...A FOOL TO GO ON LIKE THIS...WHY SHOULD I WORRY..? WHY SHOULD I *VIEW* WITH *SUSPICION?*

WELL! BEFORE I SPREADS ANY FALSE RUMORS I'LL DISCUSS IT WITH A NUMBER OF FRIENDS AND SEE WHAT *THEY* THINKS OF THE WHOLE *HORRIFYIN' STORY.*

WELL WELL, MIZ BEAVER! IS YOU GOT A MINUTE?

SORRY... HOWLAN', I IS A *BUSY* WOMAN.

NOT EVEN *THIRTY* SECONDS?

NOT *EVEN.*

150

151

It Just Ghost To Show

OH, I KNOW *OWL* HAD HIS *SHORTCOMIN'S*, BUT I DIN'T THINK IT WOULD COME TO *THIS*.

WHAT AILS YOU..?

HE WAS TELLIN' ME A *STORY* AN' KEPT GOIN' TO *SLEEP* ---SO I GOT THIS *REE*-VOLVER AN' GIVE HIM A BLAST TO MAKE HIM *WAKE UP*.

A STORY LIKE THAT JES' PLAIN INDICTS YOU *RIGHT OFF* --- SAY YOU WAS INSANE OR SAY THE GUN WENT OFF BY *ACCIDENT*.

IT *NEVER*! I DID IT ON PURPOSE.

THEN YOU GOT TO HAVE A *REASON* --I IS WILLIN' TO *SWEAR* HE WAS A *NO-GOOD, PREE*-SUMPTIOUS *BUMBLE-HEAD* WHAT WOULD OF PROVOKED HIS OWN *MOMMA* INTO *MAY-HEMMIN'* HIM.

IN?

LOOK, CHURCHY, MY LAND! I *KNOWS* YOU IS TRYIN' TO BE HELPFUL, BUT YOU GOT THIS ALL *WRONG*...

JES' TAKE IT EASY, MIZ BEAVER.

154

155

156

A CIPHER of ZEPHYRS

The Observation Post

Out behind the Pumpkin tree
The mustache of the grass
Grows green and there
          I sometime see
Rapscallions as they pass.

Their plum plumed tops
and buttons bold
And braid of burning brass
Run rattling through
the screaming gold
Of trumpets in the grass.

Flow Gently, Sweet Often

Simple Simile
Went all flimily
Going up the stair.
Said Simple Simile,
"Gosh, by Jimily,
There's a tasty air!
There's a tasty air,"
Said he,
"And there's a nasty NO!
And where's the
Cobbled keg that we
Had hidden in the snow?"

OAF OAKS AT HOME

The sentiment of cinnamon
　　Is synonym for sneeze.
The rapid rap of rhapsody
　　Is wrapping with the breeze.
The hapless hop of hoppy-toads
　　Doth trump each nightly tree.
But of the maids I ever knew
　　You're ever new to me.

Tra La for Two

Good morning,
Mary Sunshoes,
How did you wait so sood?
You've frightened off
the lulu stars
And scared away the mood.

Wash Up, Doc?

WELL NOW, FRIENDS. THIS HERE'S A MORTAR WHAT *GENERAL GRAN'MA ALLIGATOR* USED TO, *SINGLE HANDED*, FIT THE BATTLE OF *FORT MUDGE.*

BULLY FOR THE OL' GAL..

HEAR! HEAR!

NORMALLY GRAN'MA USED THIS FOR SHOOTIN' *SMOKE SIGNALS* STRAIGHT UP A MILE OR TWO ··· SHE LOVED TO TELL TALL TALES.

AN' THIS, HERR DOKTOR, I *PREE-SUME* IS THE *FUSE?*

YESSIRREE SIR ·· THAT FUSE LIES BACK AHIND THIS *CLUMMOCK* OF *HUMMOCK* AN' US'LL SET A MATCH TO IT AN' *OBSERVE* THE MORTAR FROM A SAFE *DISTINCT.*

BLESS MY EVERLOVIN' *SOFT BROWN EYES,* OL' FRIEND, BUT I DO B'LEEVE THAT IS A *WASHER MACHINE* SETTIN' THERE JES' *ACHIN'* TO WASH THESE *DUDS* OF MINE.

AN' 'LESS MY EYE-BONES DEE-CEIVE ME, MY OL' PARDNER, IT'S A *'LECTRIC WASHER MACHINE WITH CORD AT THE READY!*

NOW.. WE LIGHTS HER UP... STAYIN' BACK HERE OUTEN THE *BLAST.*

NO MATTER HOW YOU LOOKS AT IT, IT'S A *UNEASY* KIND OF NOISE FOR A WASHER TO MAKE.

'SPECIALLY IF IT TAKES YOUR BEST FRIEND WITH IT... *HOWEVER THAT AIN'T NO WASHER*... IT'S A MORTAR.

A *MORTAR?*...WHAT IN THE WORLD DOES A *MORTAR* DO?

A MORTAR GOES LIKE THIS...

BLAM

NO, IT GOES---

BOORM

NO--- IT GOES

BORAM

BOOM IS HOW IT GOES.

SUMMER SOLDIERS! WHERE YOU GOIN'?

WE'RE GOIN' TO *BOMBAY* AN' WATCH THE DAWN COME UP LIKE *THUNDER.*

165

Didn't Know It Was Loaded

168

170

The Rain of Reason

172

174

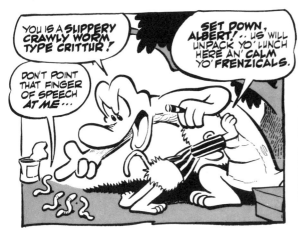

179

180

184

The Pitter Pat of Pie

THEY'S BEEN TOO MUCH *PIE-THROWIN'* GOIN' AROUN' HERE!

WHO.... *ME?*

MEBBE NOT *YOU*.... BUT MIZ BEAVER COMPLAINS THAT FOLKS BEEN *THROWIN'* HER PIES.

SOMEBODY GOT QUITE A *ARM.*

MIZ BEAVER MAKES A PERTY *POW'FUL* PIE....JES' *LIFTIN'* ONE IS USUAL ALL A MORTAL MAN KIN DO.

I DON'T KNOW WHY YOU IS SO *PREE*-JUDICED AGIN MIZ BEAVER'S PIES.... SOME OF MY *BEST FRIENDS* IS PIES....

YES....BUT WOULD YOU WANNA *MARRY* ONE? WOULD YOU WANNA *LIVE* WITH ONE....IN SICKNESS AN' IN HEALTH *'TIL DOOM DO YOU PART?*

WHY IS YOU SO *OBSESSED* WITH THOUGHTS OF *PIE?*

'CAUSE *MIZ BEAVER* IS HIRED ME TO *DEE*-LIVER 'EM FOR HER.... SHE IS STARTIN' A COMBINATION *PIE* AN' *LAUNDRY* BUSINESS....AN' NEEDS SOMEBODY *RELIABLE*....OL' BEAR AN' ALBERT *ALLUS THROWS* THE PIES....IT'S SLOPPY WORK THAT WAY.

OL' CARL ROSE

IT SOUNDS *DEE*-LIGHTFUL.... *EXCEPT* HOW KIN YOU TELL HER PIES FROM *HER* LAUNDRY?

ONE GOT A *DIFFER'NT TASTE* FROM THE *OTHER.*

187

189

WHAT-NOTS
WHAT'S NOT

WHAT NOT?

Mister Middle in the meadow,
 Riddled 'round with rain,
 Puzzle you the pitter pat
 What not goes up again?
 Riddle you the little dew
 And little do you do?
 Little did is little done,
 Tho' little did'll do.

Harken, the Hearth

Down the hill, round the rill, Pickles and Flea,
···And following fast is Fossil and me.

Leap, Lily, leap! With lumpishing jump,
Dear old Potater is caught in the pump.

But here comes Motater with scissors and twine
To cut off the coattails in time for the wine.

So it's back to the home, and home from the hunt
Come Measle and Chester and Nostril and Blunt.

To go there together to gather in glee
While the lamp of the evening
                    lights limply the lea.

The GRABBAGE of CABBAGE

It is not cricket nor cribbage nor kings
To grab at the cabbage and run around rings.

With shoemakers shooing the boot from the door
What will our Willie wash now with the floor?

The floor is a floss of flavors and flings,
So ravage the cabbage in Secular Sings.

In Secular Sings, when I was a lad,
Straw songs and whimsey were all that we had.

A View of the Mexican Boarder

The Rabbit of Easter
Is faster than few,
But quicker than quite
A quarry or two.

The Rabbit of Easter
Has eggs on the brain,
Paints them in hutches
And clutches of twain.

The Rabbit of Easter
With basket bound life
With wicker and weskit
Will weave him a wife.

The Woof Is Warped

199

WITH **HUNDERDS** OF BABY SISTERS AN' **BROTHERS**, THE HOT SPRING SUNSHINE HATCHED ME OUTEN THE LITTLE **OVAL SHELL** WHAT WAS HID IN THE SAND.

WHEN HE GO ON LIKE THIS YOU GOTTA WAIT IT OUT.

BROTHER!

THEN, ON MY CLEVER LITTLE **BABY FEET** I SCURRIED INTO THE SWAMPY WILDERNESS IN SEARCH OF FOOD.

MY DELICATE INFANT **NOSKRILS** DETECTS THE **DEE-LICORICE** ODOR OF ALL **ALLIGOMATORS'** STAFF OF LIFE... **SEE-GAR!**

SOMEWHERES I KNOWS ONE IS LURKIN'.... WAITIN' TO BE FOUND AN' **ATE.**

QUICK AN' **ALERT-LIKE** I SLITHERS AROUND! MY QUICK **CHILD-OF-THE-WILD** SENSES DIRECKS ME UNERRINGLY TO...

H'LO, ALBER... UH.... MM...

I ALWAYS LIKE THIS PART.

ME TOO... I SIT THRU IT TWICE.

HOW DARE YOU SWIPE THE ONLY FOOD OF A NEW-BORED BABE!

201

Patty-Cake
to the
Death

203

206

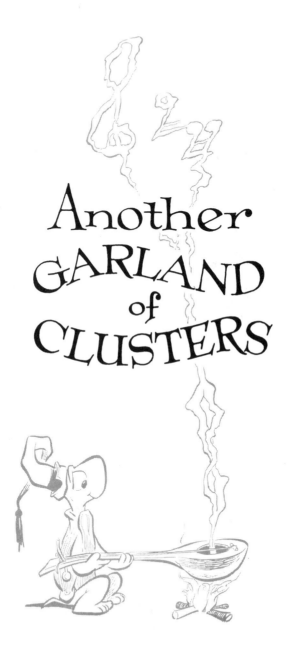

Another GARLAND of CLUSTERS

JUST ABOVE BELOW

A little a bittle beneath above
        is a little bit below
Little known to none at all,
        tho' nary knew we know.
Just before the bottom there's a
        tuppence of the top.
A hair ahead of get-to-go
        there stands the stick of stop.

✳   ✳   ✳   ✳   ✳

So quarrel the moral
        or puzzle the fuzz
The is of the will be's the wont
        of the was.

A Corner of the Circle

Around in the hoop with the loop
     of my love
  Lies longing my heart sinking low,
     thinking of
Wonders and magic and worries of woe
  With windows all waddled
     in yesterday's snow.
The sun in its tower tolls out the noon
  While here in the sphere
     of the moth-eaten moon
All huddled befuddled with night
     in the eyes
  The whoop of my heart
     in its wilderness lies.

Fiercely Fred

Fiercely Fred, the footpad dread,
  Went to Wainscoting no sooner than said.
Went to Wainscoting, Pa., did he,
  All in the Height of the Bumblebee.
"Fall with the flight of the Slumber Tree!"
  Cried Fred, the dread of the Seminaree.

"Fiercely," said Fred, with his head,
   Nodding and niddering in his bed,
"The footpad of the footpath I
   Am not so short as I am high
  Am not so high as I am wide
   I'm off with the bridle
          to rein me a bride."

A BOODLE OF BOON

Who loots my heart steals traveled trash
For, carved upon a trunk of ash
Is "Floyd Loves Flora", with a flash
Of yestereven's balderdash.

Steeple Jack
and
Stoople Jill

Of all the people on the steeple
　　None were quite so high
As Stoople Jill, who, with her bill,
　　Wrote poems on the sky.
And when her Jack did fetch her down,
　　She fetched a full fell blow
Upon his brown and crinkled crown
　　Which laid his laughter low.

Cinderola and the Fore-bears

218

219

Over His Head in a Barrel

ONE YEAR *I* WORKED AS A **DOG:** AH, I WAS NATURE'S **NOBLEST CRITTUR**-- KEEN, BOLD, HAN'SOME AN' **BRAINY.**

FIFTY THOUSAND FRENCH POSSUMS CAN'T BE WRONG -- I WAS VOTED MAM'SELLE RIGOR MORTIS OF 1903.

YOU, A **DOG?** AS MA SAID WHEN UNCLE WILLIE SKINNED A BIRCH AN' TRIED TO MAKE **SASSAMAFRASH TEA,** YOU AIN'T GOT THE **BARK** FOR THE JOB.

I DO, TOO! BE- HOLE!

BEE HOLE! THE NOBLE DOG DASHES TOWARD THE ENEMY CRYING IN A GREAT VOICE TO WIT :

RALPH! RALPH!

THAT AIN'T A **ENEMY** -- YOU IS STUCK YO' HEAD INTO A RAIN BAR'L.

RALPH?

NOW THAT YOU GOT YOUR **HEAD STUCK** IN A **BARREL** YOU PROB'LY IS GONNA LEAD A MIGHTY **SEE**-CLUDED LIFE.

DON'T BE SO HASTY -- IT MIGHT BECOME THE **HEIGHT** OF **FASHION.**

OR THE **DEPTH.**

223

IS IT DARK IN THERE?

NO, IT'S COOL AN' SMELLS OF DILL PICKLES.. ANYBODY WANNA RETIRE, **I'D** ADVISE 'EM TO GIT STUCK IN A PICKLE BARREL.

GIVE ME ANOTHER **BROCCOLI COCKTAIL** WITH A **SHOT** OF **EGGPLANT**, MINE HOST--- METHINKS I 'ESPY YON THITHER MINE OWN UGLY STEP-DAUGHTER, **CINDEROLA** WITH TWO FRIENDS' AN' A BARREL---

HO, **YOUNG WOMAN!** WHA'ST THOU HAST BEYONST IN CONTAINEST IN **PRIVY HOLD** WITHIN THY **BARREL,** 'EY, DAUGHTER LOVE?

CRUEL STEPMA, YOU'M HAD **TOO MANY STRAWBERRIES** -- YOU SOUND LIKE A LOAD OF COAL.

E'EN SO, ALBEIT AN' PRIVY COUNCIL THE LATTERMOST! ANOTHER **CUCUMBER SQUEEZE** WITH A **DASH OF ENDIVE**, MY DEAR --- I'LL WAGER A PRETTY THAT YOUR BARREL WILL BEAR LOOKING INTO.

AN' IT BEARS LOOKIN' **OUT** OF, TOO, MEIN-HEER.

NOW THEN, WHAT DO YOU AN' YOUR TWO LITTLE FRIENDS GOT IN THE BARREL? ---WITH SUCH GOIN'S ON, WHERE DO YOU EXPECK TO GET--- **A HEAD!?**

A HEAD! A HEAD! IN THE BARREL! A HEAD IN THE BARREL!

WE BETTER **SNOOTCH** OFF! MAKIN' OUT WE IS A **POO-RADE!**

225

Pumpin' Pumpkins

229

The Air Is Thin on Top

232

233

I'LL PUT IT DOWN **SO** -- THEN I'LL TROMP AT IT UNTIL IT'S ALL **SMOOTH** -- AN' THIN AS A COAT OF PAINT.

FIRST I STARTS WITH A **FLYIN' STOMP** --

CRUNK!

HOO HOO! *HO, THERE! HALLOO!* WELL, THERE GOES A GOOD KID -- BRIGHT, ALERT, EAGER AN' TWO OF THE **BIGGEST** FEET IN THE KINGDOM.

THING FOR ME TO DO NOW IS FIND ANOTHER PUNKIN ····

WELL, I **TROW!** THERE'S THE **GOOD WIFE** NOW ···· EMERGING FROM YON **GAS COMPANY MANHOLE** -

SORRY, GENIE, THAT AIR GOT DRUV **SO DEEP** YOU COULDN'T FIND IT WITH A **GEIGER COUNTER** AN' A **TEAM OF GOPHERS.**

Ugly as a Bugly in a Rugly

239

240

242

DOES YOU MEAN I IS *NOT A BEAUTIFUL* STEP MOMMA?

YUP.

WODDYA MEAN "YUP"?

THE MINUTE I LOOKED AT YOU I *KNOWED* YOU WAS A GAL WHAT WAS *TRUE AN' BLUE* IN HEART, IN MIND, IN BODY, IN SPIRIT, IN CHICAGO AND···

HOW COULD A LOVELY CRITTUR EVER FORGIVE ME IF I DIN'T TREAT HER WITH THE UTMOST INTEGERTY AN' STUFF LIKE THAT··· *LIPS WHAT TELLS LIES WILL NEVER TOUCH HER CRAMBERRY PIE, I SAID.*

SO···I KNOW YO' HEART OF GOLD WILL BE *REE-FRESHED···REE-*STORED *AND REE-*JUVENATED TO HEAR ME SAY: *'YES, YOU AIN'T A BEAUTIFUL STEP MOMMA!*

JES' FER THAT, *NO CRAMBERRY PIE FOR YOU.*

I HATES CRAMBERRY PIE AND I IS GONE TAKE OUT A LICENSE TO *HATE YOU.*

ME AN' CRAMBERRY PIE HATES YOU BACK.

243

The Trip of the Light Fantastic

Shoe
Fly
Pie
R2

252

IF I HAD MY WAY, I'D WOUND YOU TO THE *DEAD*, TOO... YO' *MAGICAL* POWERS IS BLOWED A *FUSE.*

ARGH!

HERE I IS LOOKIN' FOR *CINDEROLA* AN' DOIN' A BETTER JOB WITH A *SHOE* ON MY HEAD THAN YOU IS WITH ALL YO' *TRICKS.*

A SHOE ON YO' HEAD! THAT GIVE MY QUICK TRIGGERED LI'L' OL' LOYAL HARD WORKIN' BRAIN A *BIG FAT IDEA!*

IN-AN'-ASMUCH AS THEM *SHOES* YOU GOT IS *CINDEROLA'S* DAINTY LI'L' *SLIPPERS,* US KIN FIND THE GAL FO' YOU, PRINCE, BY FITTIN' THE SHOES TO THE MAIDENS OF YO' *EVER LOVIN' KINGDOM.*

GREAT! FOR SUCH CLEAR BRAINED THINKIN' I IS GONE PLACE YOU WITH MY *CEMETERY DEPARTMINT* SOON AS THEY IS A *DOGBONED OPENIN'!*

GLAD YOU *DIGS* ME!

HURRY! THEY IS NOT A MINUTE TO LOSE---

AYE SIRE, SIR, YOUR MAJESTY OL' BOY, PAL.

BE *HOLE!* THAT HOUSE THERE GOT A LOOK ON HER LIKE IT MIGHT CONTAIN A BEVY OF BEAUTIFUL GALS.

LET'S TRY THERE, F. GODMOMMA, OL' SPORT.

The End
(of Cinderola
and all that)

And what is the happy ending
When the foot fits the shoe?
And where are the knightly wending
In the vast blasts of blue,
Tracking up clean tomorrows
In search of a bright today,
Counting their well-worn sorrows
In the hope they'll go away?